Essential Question
What do myths help us understand?

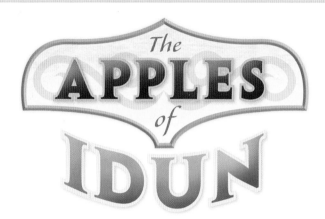

The **APPLES** *of* **IDUN**

adapted by Betsy Hebert

illustrated by Valeria Cis

Chapter 1

THE EAGLE

Long ago, the **gods** lived on Earth. One day, Loki and Odin were in the woods. The two gods were hungry.

Odin killed an ox. Loki made a fire. But the meat would not cook.

Was this a trick? Loki looked around. No one **appeared**.

Then Loki looked up. He saw an eagle in a tree.

The eagle said, "I will cook the meat if you will share it."

"Yes, have some meat," Odin said.

The meat cooked. Then the eagle **swooped** down. He grabbed most of the meat. This made Loki angry. So he hit the eagle with a large stick.

The eagle grabbed the stick. Now Loki could not let go of it. He was stuck! That's because this was not a real eagle. It was a storm giant in the shape of an eagle.

STOP AND CHECK

Who is the eagle?

THE APPLES

The eagle flew off with Loki. "Let me go," Loki **begged**.

The eagle said, "I will let you go if you do this one thing for me. I want the apples of Idun and you must get them."

Loki said, "I can't do that!"

The goddess Idun goddess grew beautiful **golden** apples. These were special apples. Eating them kept the gods young.

Loki was tired and hurt. At last he said, "I will get you the apples."

So the eagle dropped Loki.

STOP AND CHECK

Why are the apples special?

Loki went to see Idun. "Those are beautiful apples," Loki told her.

"There are no others like them," replied Idun. "They keep the gods young."

Loki said, "I saw a tree with apples just like those at the edge of the city."

"Show me this tree," Idun said.

"Okay," said Loki. "Bring some apples. Then we can **compare** them."

STOP AND CHECK

What does Loki tell Idun?

Chapter 3

THE CHASE

Idun filled her basket with apples, and they left the city. Just then, the eagle storm giant flew down. He snatched Idun. In **moments**, they were gone.

The next day, the gods waited for their apples. But Idun did not come. The gods **searched** for her. Days went by. Without the apples, the gods began to grow old.

STOP AND CHECK

What happened to the gods without Idun's apples?

Then the gods found out that
Loki had tricked Idun. They were
very angry.

Loki said, "I'm sorry! I will get her
back." He used his powers to turn
into a falcon. He flew to the storm
giant's house.

Loki found Idun. He turned the
goddess and her apples into nuts.
Loki put the nuts into Idun's basket.
Then he flew off with it.

But the storm giant saw Loki. He
flew after him.

The gods saw Loki coming. They made piles of wood. The gods lit the wood on fire after Loki flew into the city.

The eagle could not fly through the fire. They were safe. Idun was a goddess again. She fed the gods, and they grew young. Loki had fixed his **mistake**!

STOP AND CHECK

How did Loki get the apples back?

Respond to Reading

Summarize

Summarize *The Apples of Idun.* Use the chart to help you.

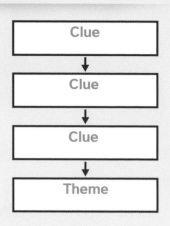

Text Evidence

1. What is the message of this myth?

   Theme

2. Reread page 13. How can you tell what kind of animal a *falcon* is?

   Vocabulary

3. Write about what Loki did in the beginning of the story. What did he do in the end? Write About Reading

Compare Texts
Read about another golden fruit.

Tomatoes

Tomatoes come
in many colors.

FoodCollection

flower

fruit

fruit

stem

Tomatoes **develop** in **stages**.
A yellow flower grows. The flower
becomes a tomato. At first it is
green. Then the tomato gets ripe.
It turns red or yellow.

18

Illustration: Rob Schuster

Tomatoes came from South America. Now tomatoes grow around the world. Large **crops** of tomatoes are grown in the United States.

Tomatoes are good cooked and raw.

How to Grow Tomatoes

1. Put a pot of tomato seeds and soil in a sunny window.

2. Give the seeds water. After six weeks, move the plants outside.

3. Put them in a bigger pot or in the ground. You'll have tomatoes in about three months!

Make Connections

What did Loki learn? Essential Question

How is a yellow tomato like one of Idun's apples? Text to Text

Focus on
Genre

Myth A myth is a type of folktale. Many myths have gods or goddesses. They explain things about the world.

What to Look for The characters in *The Apples of Idun* are gods and goddesses. They have special powers. Idun grows golden apples that keep the gods young.

Your Turn

Plan a myth about a god or goddess. Give your character a name. Tell what special things he or she can do.